AN ILLUSTRATED TOUR
Color Your Way Through New England's Covered Bridges

SANBORN BRIDGE

NATIONAL SOCIETY FOR THE PRESERVATION OF COVERED BRIDGES

with Courtney Parsons and Heidi Smith

An Illustrated Tour
Color Your Way Through New England's Covered Bridges

Library of Congress Control Number: 2022916668

Paperback ISBN: 979-8-9854340-7-1

Book Cover, Design and Layout: Courtney Parsons

Editor: Jane Stucker

Book Collaborator: Heidi Smith

Give a Salute! provides publishing services to the author(s) specifications and approval. The author retains all responsibilities and rights to the content of this book.

NATIONAL SOCIETY FOR THE PRESERVATION OF COVERED BRIDGES

HELP PRESERVE OUR HERITAGE
www.coveredbridgesociety.org

Color Your Way USA

IN MEMORY OF RICHARD SANDERS ALLEN

1917-2008

Most of the great men of the covered bridge world were involved directly with building, but one was a scholar: Richard Sanders Allen.

In 1937, at the age of twenty, Rick developed his lifelong interest in covered bridges. He was never one to do anything halfway. He began corresponding with state and county engineers and historians to gather as much information as he could on existing and former covered bridges.

His research enhanced, and often corrected, previously known information. His many books on the topic were written to share covered bridge history in a way that appeals to the general public.

In April 1943, he started printing a newsletter called *Covered Bridge Topics* to share his research with a more scholarly audience. As the caretakers of Rick's research and his collection of photographs, we gratefully dedicate this book to him.

Richard Sanders Allen Collection, NSPCB Archives

ABOUT THE AUTHORS
THE NSPCB

On March 7, 1950, Leo Litwin (1909-1987) and George B. Pease (1899-1961) hosted the first meeting of covered bridge hobbyists in the Boston area with 16 people in attendance. They spent the evening sharing photos and stories of their travels to covered bridges. By the end of the same year, the group evolved into the "Society for the Preservation of Covered Bridges" (SPCB), with Litwin as president and Pease as Secretary-Treasurer.

Photo by Bob Watts

During the summer of 1954, the group incorporated as the National Society for the Preservation of Covered Bridges, Inc. The charter listed the Society's purpose as:

- To preserve covered bridges.
- To gather and record knowledge of the history of covered bridges.
- To collect and preserve pictures, printed and manuscript matter, and other articles of historical interest concerning covered bridges.
- To do all things, alone or in cooperation with other persons or corporations, necessary or advisable to carry out any or all of the foregoing purposes and objects.

Presently, more covered bridges are lost to arson than any other cause. Some bridges are outfitted with fire alarms, fire retardants, and fire suppression systems to reduce the potential for destruction. To help with this effort, the NSPCB has a program to provide fire retardant for historic covered bridges.

Monthly meetings are held between March and October, except in May. Membership includes copies of two quarterly publications. Covered Bridge Topics, founded in 1943 by noted researcher Richard Sanders Allen, includes in-depth articles about existing and former bridges. The Newsletter contains current bridge news along with information about upcoming events. The NSPCB also offers a World Guide to Covered Bridges listing covered wood-truss bridges worldwide. The most recent edition was published in the fall of 2021.

More information about the NSPCB, including membership details, is available at: www.coveredbridgesociety.org.

NATIONAL SOCIETY FOR THE
PRESERVATION OF COVERED BRIDGES

HELP PRESERVE OUR HERITAGE
www.coveredbridgesociety.org

INTRODUCTION

Background

Covered bridges are known to have existed in China for over 2,000 years. It is not currently known how many exist there, but it is believed there are over 3,000. Chinese covered bridges are gathering places, not just a means to cross the river. The interior of the bridge may also include shrines, vendors and benches to sit on and socialize. In Europe, covered bridges date back to the Middle Ages. About 550 still stand there, with about 85% of them in Austria, Germany or Switzerland.

In the early 1800s in America, horses and wagons typically crossed smaller streams at fords which were not safe during times of high water. Large river crossings often depended on ferries which could be very dangerous and unreliable due to flooding, storms and winter ice. Early bridges were either stone, which was expensive and difficult to work with, or crude wooden bridges. Being uncovered, the wooden ones only lasted a few years before the wood deteriorated.

Due to the expense of building a fully covered bridge, the earliest ones in America were grand structures over large rivers, which warranted the additional expense of protecting the investment by adding a roof and boarding sides. This protected the structural trusses from the elements, thus extending their potential lifespan. Within a few years, even the smaller crossings would be covered, and the covered bridge became a common sight throughout much of the country. Most early bridges were designed by architects and built by local carpenters. The ever-increasing need to create longer spans and carry heavier loads encouraged development of stronger truss designs. By the end of the 19th century, iron was more readily

Acknowledgements

Information for the New Hampshire bridges in this book was obtained from Covered Bridges of New Hampshire (2022) by Kim Varney Chandler. Notes from other states were obtained from Covered Spans of Yesteryear, www.lostbridges.org. Thanks to Scott Wagner, Bob Watts, Kim Chandler, Arnold & Meg Graton and Bill & Jenn Caswell for their assistance in selecting the photos and preparing the text for this book. Thanks to Give A Salute! /Color Your Way USA for the opportunity to see it published.

Covered Bridges

When one first develops an interest in covered bridges, it is difficult to know where to start. They appeal to people in many different ways. For some, they hold memories of childhood, summers swimming under the bridge, or weekend drives in the country. For others, it is the quality of the construction which has allowed them to carry traffic for over 100 years. Photographers admire the artistic qualities of the landscape surrounding the bridge while others cherish the history that they represent.

Like most other historic artifacts, covered bridges have something to teach us about our past. When they were originally constructed, they represented advanced technology in bridge construction. They were often built by local carpenters who were respected members of their community.

Today, they offer us a glimpse of what life was like a century and a half ago. You can walk up to them, touch them, examine them, and learn from them. Many areas promote their covered bridges as tourist attractions to

bring visitors into the area which helps support the local economy. available and becoming the material of choice for larger bridge projects.

As iron, and later, concrete and steel, became more popular, wooden covered bridges were routinely replaced except in timber-rich areas like Oregon, Québec and New Brunswick, which continued building them until the 1950s

The rapid disappearance from the landscape prompted the creation of a number of organizations devoted to preserving those which remain. Some areas also saw the economic potential of building new covered bridges to attract visitors to their regions. Sometimes those new structures were constructed as replicas of historic bridges being replaced, and some were entirely new.

The attraction of covered bridges has also encouraged some to be built by individuals on their private property, in parks, on golf courses, etc.

The 2021 edition of the *World Guide to Covered Bridges* lists a combined total of 179 wooden-truss covered bridges within the New England states.

Connecticut - 7 + 1 boxed pony
Maine - 8 + 1 boxed pony
Massachusetts - 10
New Hampshire - 55 + 3 boxed pony
New Hampshire & Vermont - 3
Rhode Island - 0
Vermont - 96

Total: 179 + 5 boxed pony

TERMINOLOGY

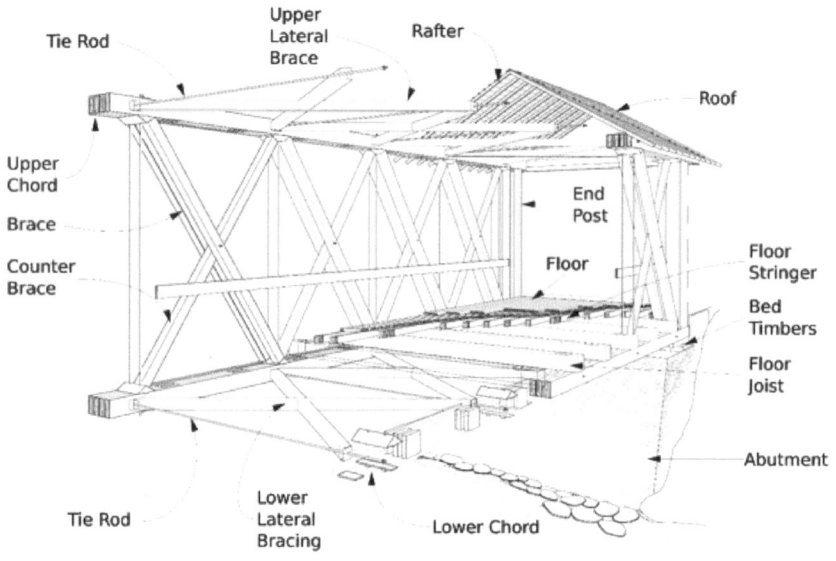

Diagram adapted from one created by Lola Bennett, Thomas Behrens, Charu Chaudhry, and Christopher H. Marston, 2006. Note that not all terms listed below are shown on the diagram.

DEFINITIONS

Abutment: The foundation supporting the bridge at both ends.

Arch: A curved structural member spanning an opening and serving as a support.

Bed Timbers: Timber components typically located between the top of an abutment or pier and the underside of the lower chord. Intended to serve as sacrificial components, they are easily replaced when deteriorated by rot, thus protecting truss components from similar deterioration.

Boxed Pony Truss: A bridge supported by short trusses which are typically covered on both sides. Because of their shorter height, these structures do not have a roof.

Brace: Diagonal member in a truss slanting upward toward the center or midpoint of the truss providing structural support.

Camber: The vertical curvature of a bridge rising upward towards the center to help eliminate sagging.

Counter Brace: A diagonal timber in a truss which slants in the opposite direction from the brace.

Dead Load: The weight of materials that make up the bridge structure itself.

Floor Joist: Timbers running across the bottom of the bridge supporting the floor planks. Sometimes referred to as deck beams.

Flooring or Decking: Planks resting on or secured to the floor beams which form the bridge floor.

Floor Stringer: If used, they span between the floor beams with the flooring or decking on top of them.

End Post: The outermost vertical post of a truss which transfers the load supported by the truss to the abutment.

Lower Lateral Bracing: Cross bracing at the bottom of the trusses to resist excessive loads or wind pressure.

Lower Chord or Bottom Chord: The timbers running the bottom length of the truss.

Panel: A repeated section of the truss. Typically, the area between two adjacent vertical posts.

Pier: A support in midstream between the two abutments.

Portal: The entrance at each end of a bridge.

Post: A vertical timber connecting the lower and upper chords.

Rafter: Diagonal member supporting the roofing. In most examples they rest on the upper chord.

Roof: Structure atop the trusses to protect them from weather.

Shelter Panel: A short section of siding inside the ends of the bridge, to protect the truss ends from damage due to rain.

Siding: Vertical or horizontal exterior covering to protect the trusses from weather.

Span: The distance between adjacent supports, or a section of a bridge.

Tie Rod: Metal rods connecting two upper or lower chords, or securing a bridge to an abutment.

Treenails: Pronounced "trunnels." The wooden pins driven into the holes in planks of a lattice truss to fasten them together. Treenails are made of hardwood, usually oak.

Upper Chord or Top Chord: The timbers running the top length of the truss.

Upper Lateral Bracing: Cross bracing at the top of the trusses to resist excessive loads or wind pressure.

TRUSS DESIGNS

The truss is an essential part of the support system for the covered bridge. The type of truss is often used for categorizing bridges. Some designs see extensive use over a large geographical area, while others are limited to a specific region. Simplified descriptions and line drawings of the most common designs follow. There are many examples of variations, modifications, and refinements to these truss designs.

The most basic design is the **Kingpost** truss which has been used since the Middle Ages. It is based on an equilateral triangle with a central post, known as the kingpost. It is used for short bridges up to about 40' long.

The **Queenpost** truss is an expansion of the Kingpost design, adding a rectangular panel in between the two triangles. This design has been in use at least as far back as the Italian Renaissance. It was typically used to span distances up to 75' long.

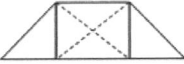

The **Multiple Kingpost** truss is an expansion of the Kingpost truss. The diagonal timbers carry the load from the center of the bridge outward to each successive vertical Kingpost which transfers it to the next diagonal timber. It is useful for spans up to about 100' long.

Theodore Burr (1771-1822) was an inventor from Torrington, Connecticut, who patented his **Burr** truss designs in 1806 and 1817. It was essentially a Multiple Kingpost design combined with an arch with ends seated against the abutments below the lower chords. Today, about one-quarter of the remaining historic covered bridges use this design.

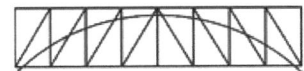

Ithiel Town (1784–1844) of New Haven, Connecticut, was an architect who, in 1820, patented a truss bridge consisting of two layers of overlapping planks forming a lattice fastened together with wooden pins called "treenails" at each intersection. **Town** trusses are erected with sawn planks instead of heavy hewn timbers, making the timbers somewhat easier to work with. Today, about one-quarter of the remaining historic covered bridges use this design.

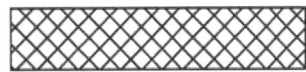

Col. Stephen H. Long (1784–1864) is best known for his surveys as an engineer in the U.S. Army Topographical Engineers. He became interested in the design and construction of bridges patenting his **Long** truss design in 1830. Very few Long truss bridges remain, primarily in Maine and New Hampshire.

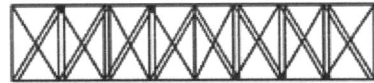

William Howe of Massachusetts, designed the **Howe** truss and patented it in 1840. By substituting adjustable iron rods for the wooden posts of the Long truss, Howe's design was much stronger, making it very popular for railroad bridges. Those in the eastern states typically have wooden diagonal braces in both directions, forming an "X". Ones in western states typically only have braces angled upward towards the center of the bridge. Howe trusses were also popular in parts of Europe, where some still stand in Austria, Germany and Switzerland.

Robert W. Smith (1834–1898) of Ohio, received patents for his **Smith** truss designs in 1867 and 1869. He continued to modify and refine his designs without applying for additional patents. As a result, many Smith truss bridges do not exactly follow the patented designs. The variety makes categorizing them somewhat challenging.

Peter Paddleford (1785-1859) of Littleton, New Hampshire, was a bridge builder who developed the **Paddleford** truss. Although Paddleford never patented his design, it dominated covered bridge construction throughout northern New England for over half a century. Examples of this design are found in northeastern Vermont, northern New Hampshire, and northwestern Maine.

Many more designs exist beyond those described in this limited space. Hopefully, this short section kindled your interest and prompts you to learn more about the designs and builders.

COVER PHOTO
STARK BRIDGE - STARK, NH

The Stark Bridge is one of the most photographed, illustrated, and painted covered bridges in New Hampshire. It was reportedly built around 1862, and is one of twenty-two Paddleford truss bridges remaining in the world. In 1895, a spring freshet tore the two-span bridge from its abutments and floated it downstream. Local men sawed the bridge in sections and hauled it upstream via wagon. The bridge was then reinstalled without a center pier.

The Stark Bridge received repairs in 1919 and 1940; major repairs in 1954 included reinstalling a center pier. In 2014, the Stark Bridge received $1.4 million in repairs, partially funded by the National Historic Covered Bridge Preservation Program. The project was awarded a Preservation Achievement Award by the New Hampshire Preservation Alliance and an Engineering Excellence Awards Competition National Recognition Award by the American Council of Engineering Companies in 2016.

Fun Fact: In 1947, the Stark Bridge was in bad shape, and the town was considering replacing it. The deliberation to remove the historic bridge caught the attention of state lawmakers. On May 15, 1947, the New Hampshire State Senate passed Senate Joint Resolution No. 9, appropriating state funding to repair the beloved landmark.

Bull's Bridge - Kent, CT

Bull's Bridge in Kent, Connecticut, was named after Jacob Bull of Dover Plains, New York, who built the first bridge at this site in the 1770s. The original bridge was primarily built to aid in transporting iron from the furnaces in the Kent area to the Hudson River. The bridge standing at the site today was originally a toll bridge that was built in 1842, at a cost of $3000.

When the main dam of the Connecticut Light and Power Company was built in 1901-03, the bridge had to be raised 20 feet to remain clear of the water. It was restored in 1949, to remove a noticeable sag and replace split and rotted bottom chords.

Fun Fact: There have been stories over the years that the covered bridge was built in 1778, and was crossed by George Washington in 1781. Although Washington visited the area, and could have passed over Bull's Bridge, it would have been an earlier bridge at this location since the truss design used in this one was not developed until 1820.

Photo from the Richard Sanders Allen Collection, NSPCB Archives

West Cornwall or Hart's Bridge - West Cornwall, CT

While some sources list the West Cornwall Bridge's construction date as 1841, it was more likely constructed in 1864, at the western edge of West Cornwall, Connecticut. It has been said that the West Cornwall Bridge was originally built as a single span structure with the center pier being added in 1924, to provide extra strength. However, the Cornwall Historical Society has a 1913 photograph of the bridge showing this extra pier. It was also called Hart's Bridge after an early settler in the area. Early pictures show squared portals that were replaced with more typical gable entryways during repairs in 1946. The West Cornwall Bridge is Connecticut's longest covered bridge and has an unusual truss design, a Town truss sandwiched in between two Queenpost trusses. It is similar in design to the Bull's Bridge.

Fun Fact: During the winter of 1960-61, the bridge was threatened by an ice jam. On February 26, 1961, the ice was dynamited, and the water level dropped back below the bridge.

Photo by David Wray

Porter-Parsonsfield Bridge - ME

The first bridge at Porter Village was completed around 1800, and replaced in 1808. The 152-foot-long Porter-Parsonsfield Bridge was built over the Ossipee River by the towns of Porter and Parsonsfield as a joint project. It is interesting to note that a plaque on the bridge indicates it was built in 1876, but other sources list the construction date as 1859.

A town history, written in 1879, states that the covered bridge at Porter Village was built "in 1876, costing this town $1,717.24." Construction of the bridge has been credited to Jacob H. Berry (1827–1892). It is the only Maine covered bridge that connects two counties, as Porter is in Oxford County and Parsonsfield is in York County. Many substantial repairs and renovations have occurred over the years, leaving little of the original bridge intact. Enhancements included that addition of large laminated wooden arches. Cables are attached and secured to the shore to provide support during flood times. The bridge was closed to traffic in 1960, when the new bridge was built upstream, and it is currently open to pedestrian traffic only. It was listed on the National Register of Historic Places on February 16, 1970.

Fun Fact: There is a story of a dispute over the costs of building and maintaining the bridge when it was to be constructed. A group of selectmen from each town met on the old uncovered span. The meeting culminated when a selectman from Parsonsfield took a jackknife and tossed it at the midpoint of the span. He proceeded to say "the Town of Parsonsfield shall build so far and no further!"

Photo by C. Ernest Walker Photo, NSPCB Archives

Robyville Bridge - ME

The Robyville Bridge was built over Kenduskeag Stream in Corinth, Maine, in 1872, and is the last remaining historic covered bridge in Penobscot County. The cost of the bridge was $1375.06, and it was built by Royal A. Sweet (1837-1905) who, in addition to being a carpenter, was also recognized as a blacksmith and carriage maker. It is also thought that the timbers used in its construction were most likely hauled by oxen by Royal from George Palmer's mill in the Town of Garland. Steel beams were added in 1983, to carry the live load.

The bridge is a rare example of a Long truss bridge. The Long truss was developed and patented by Col. Stephen Harriman Long (1784 – 1864), who undertook numerous projects for the U.S. Army Topographical Engineers, surveying sites for canals and leading expeditions in the West. As a consulting engineer for the Baltimore & Ohio Railroad, Long became interested in the design and construction of bridges. In 1830, he obtained a patent for a wooden truss bridge with diagonal compression members and vertical tension members and received patents for variations on this design in 1836 and 1839. Central to Long's patented design was the concept of driving wedges into the connections, which prestressed the structure, ensuring that the compression and tension members functioned efficiently.

Fun Fact: Robeyville (now spelled Robyville) is a village within the town of Corinth, Maine. It was named after Samuel Robey, who owned a large gristmill in the area.

Photo by Bill & Jenn Caswell

Burkeville Bridge - Conway, MA

This bridge is also known as the Conway Bridge. The first bridge at this location is thought to have been built in 1850. The great flood of early October 1869 swept away ten bridges on the South River between the Ashfield town line and Deerfield River. The bridge at this location was one of two which remained; both of them were left impassable. At the annual town meeting on May 21, 1870, voters approved a request to rebuild the bridge. Local carpenter Sylvanus P. Sherman (1826-1912) led the crew building the new bridge. Town records show payments for the construction from August 1870 until May 1871. The bridge was damaged by the September 1938 hurricane and restricted to light traffic until repairs were made in 1940.

In 1983, the bridge was considered unsafe and closed to all traffic. Restoration was plagued by a series of delays. The bridge was finally renovated in 2004 and 2005 by Stan Graton's 3G Construction. When the work was finished, the state advised the bridge stay closed to vehicle traffic due to its lack of steel and crash-tested guardrails. In July 2013, the Massachusetts Department of Transportation informed the town it was the town's decision whether it wanted to open the bridge to traffic. After consulting the police chief and highway superintendent, the Selectboard voted to open the bridge to vehicle traffic for the first time in 28 years. On November 17, 2013, a celebration was held to re-open the bridge to vehicle traffic.

Fun Fact: After the ceremony to re-open the bridge, the town's oldest resident, Helen Reed, 97, was the first one to ride through it in an open horse-drawn carriage driven by Amanda Kantor.

Photo by Bill & Jenn Caswell

Gilbertville Bridge - Gilbertville, MA

This bridge is also known as the Hardwick-Ware Bridge and Bridge Street Bridge. It was built over the Ware River in the factory village of Gilbertville in 1886. The village within the town of Hardwick was centered around a wool textile mill that was founded in the 1860s, by George H. Gilbert, who already had wool factories in nearby Ware on the Ware River. When the mill complex was expanded further to the south, the covered bridge was built to connect it to the road between Gilbertville and Ware on the west side of the river. At that location, the Ware River is also the town line between Hardwick in Worcester County and Ware in Hampshire County. Extensive repairs were made in 1986. The bridge was closed again in 2002, and reopened in 2011, after repairs were completed. Those repairs included the addition of steel I-beams under the deck to carry the weight of traffic. The bridge was listed on the National Register of Historic Places on May 8, 1986.

Fun Fact: The towns of Hardwick and Ware shared ownership of the bridge and did not always coordinate repairs to the structure. That is evident in this photo taken from the Hardwick side of the river by Henry A. Gibson on July 17, 1948.

Photo by Henry A. Gibson, NSPCB Archives

Bath Bridge - Bath, NH

Photo by Philippe H. Bonnet, NSPCB Archives

At 375' long, the Bath Bridge is the longest covered bridge entirely within the state of New Hampshire. The current structure is the fifth bridge on this site across the Ammonoosuc River and was built in 1832. In 1833, the town posted signs reading, "One dollar fine to drive any team faster than a walk on this bridge." Not only was this a town ordinance, but also the New Hampshire legislature passed an act that same year ensuring the fine. In 1835, the town of Bath voted that the bridge could not be used as a horse shed, as local folks would tie up their horses inside the bridge when they came to town. In 1853, the White Mountain Railroad laid tracks underneath the Bath Bridge. The bridge was renovated in 1918, and new hemlock arches were installed. In 1987, master bridgewright Arnold M. Graton renovated the bridge again. It was closed in 2012 for a $2.92 million renovation by Wright Construction Co., Inc. and reopened on August 14, 2014.

Fun Fact: In 1987, when Graton removed the interior wainscoting, several chewed-up posts, some chewed straight through, was revealed. It seems the town had a good reason for prohibiting the bridge from being used as a stable. Tied up horses, bored and hungry, made themselves a meal out of the bridge posts. The posts are visible today.

Contoocook Railroad Bridge - Hopkinton, NH

Built in 1889, the Contoocook Railroad Bridge replaced an earlier span built in 1850. This double Town lattice truss bridge was made from locally-sourced eastern spruce and designed to carry heavier trains. The bridge was washed off the abutments during the Great Flood of 1936 but, fortunately was kept from becoming down-river scrap wood as the railroad tracks were bolted together at each joint. The bridge was picked up and put back on the abutments by the railroad crews, only to be damaged two years later by the Great Hurricane of 1938. By 1962, rail travel ended along the line, and the bridge was used as a warehouse until 1990 when it was given to the New Hampshire Division of Historic Resources (NHDHR). In 2006, the bridge received $110,000 worth of repairs funded through the National Society for the Preservation of Covered Bridges Eastman Thomas Fund.

Fun Fact: There are seven fully covered railroad bridges remaining in the world, and five are located in New Hampshire. The Contoocook Railroad Bridge is the oldest surviving covered railroad bridge in the world.

Photo from the Richard E. Roy Collection, NSPCB Archives

Corbin Bridge - Newport, NH

Dr. James Corbin settled in North Newport around 1790 and owned the property on which the bridge was built. The first covered bridge in this location, over the north branch of the Sugar River, was built in 1843 by Anson Warren. That bridge was maintained by the Town of Newport until it was destroyed by arson on May 25, 1993. Utilizing insurance proceeds and private fundraising, the town hired master bridgewright Arnold M. Graton of Holderness to recreate their beloved covered bridge. Using as many authentic building techniques as possible, Graton invited the community to participate in the construction. The bridge was pulled across the river by a team of oxen during a three-day, nineteenth-century-style festival with almost nine thousand people in attendance. Graton and his crew finished construction through the cold fall and winter, and the new Corbin Bridge opened on January 8, 1995. In 2021, Graton returned to the bridge to replace the roof.

Fun Fact: In 2018, two partially-burned large beams of southern yellow pine from the original Corbin Bridge were recovered on the banks of the Sugar River. After drying in a barn for ten months, the end of one beam was cut off to count the rings. It is estimated these trees were planted sometime in the 1660s.

Photo by Henry A. Gibson, NSPCB Archives

Cornish - Windsor Bridge - Cornish, NH, and Windsor, VT

Photo by C. Ernest Walker, NSPCB Archives

At 460' long, the Cornish-Windsor Bridge is the longest historic wooden-truss bridge in the United States and the longest two-span covered bridge in the world. It is the fourth bridge in this location spanning the Connecticut River. The first two bridges, built in 1796 and 1824, were destroyed by floods; the third bridge, built in 1849, was destroyed by an ice floe in 1866. The current bridge was built the same year by James Tasker and Bela Fletcher who framed the bridge in a meadow and reassembled it over the river. The bridge was paid for by tolls collected at the toll house on the Vermont side of the river until 1943. The Cornish-Windsor Bridge was briefly closed for repairs in 1925, 1929, 1936, 1938, and 1954. Due to safety concerns, the bridge closed in 1987. It reopened in December 1989, after a $4.4 million restoration by Chesterfield Associates. The bridge is a National Historic Civil Engineering Landmark.

Fun Fact: Toll keeper James Monteith kept a close eye on Saturday night travelers. Pedestrians in the dry town of Windsor utilized the bridge to frequent the saloon in Cornish. He charged two cents to get into New Hampshire and three cents to return to Vermont. If Monteith wasn't familiar with the man, or if he knew him too well, he demanded the return toll in advance.

Flume Bridge - Franconia State Park, NH

Photo by Scott Wagner

The Flume Bridge is located in Franconia State Park and is accessible along a two-mile walking loop through the Flume Gorge. The carriage road at this location across the Pemigewasset River was laid out in 1871, by the Lincoln Turnpike Company. There was undoubtedly a bridge here; it is uncertain whether or not it was covered, but it was more than likely damaged by the Flume Slide of 1883. A sign on the current Flume Bridge indicates 1886 as the year of construction.

Between 1971 and 1983, steel girders were added under the wooden truss for support. In 2009, the stone retaining wall adjacent to the bridge and one of the abutments were repaired. The Flume Bridge is maintained by the New Hampshire Department of Natural and Cultural Resources and is one of twenty-two Paddleford truss bridges remaining.

Fun Fact: The Flume Bridge, and the surrounding 5,500 acres in the notch, were privately owned until 1928, when they were sold to the state of New Hampshire. At the time, 913 acres were deeded to the Society for the Protection of New Hampshire Forests (SPNHF) to operate as Flume Reservation. In 1947, the SPNHF transferred ownership back to the state, where it became part of Franconia Notch State Park.

Jackson Bridge - Jackson, NH

The Jackson Bridge, or Honeymoon Bridge, was built across the Ellis River around 1876, by local dairy farmer Charles Broughton and his son, Frank. Because Broughton could not be away from his farm for too long, he would assemble bridges on his property. He would draw elaborate plans of the bridge, mark each piece with carved numbers, disassemble the pieces, then transport and reassemble the pieces at the bridge location. Broughton used ship's knees (naturally curved pieces of wood) for bracing and made his own nails by hand. He exclusively utilized the truss design of Peter Paddleford. A pedestrian sidewalk was added in 1930, and repairs were made in 1965, and 1984. A $1 million rehabilitation was made to the Jackson Bridge in 2002 by CCS Constructors and was partially funded by the National Historic Covered Bridge Preservation Program.

Fun Fact: The term "Honeymoon Bridge" first appears in print in a 1936 essay published in the New Hampshire Troubadour and written by bridge historian Adelbert M. Jakeman (1905–1983).

". . . there is one (covered bridge) that will always remain in our memory, literally, 'till death do us part.' That is the beautiful bridge over the Ellis River at Jackson. It might well be named Honeymoon Bridge. On our wedding night, and on the threshold of a new life, as it were, we strolled arm and arm through the sheltering shadows of this ancient rustic bridge and lingered beneath its rude protecting roof" (J. D. Conwill 1993).

Photo by Bob Watts

Sulphite Bridge - Franklin, NH

The Sulphite Railroad Bridge is one of seven historic covered railroad bridges left in the world and is the only surviving deck truss covered bridge in the United States. It was constructed in 1896 by the Boston & Maine Railroad as part of the line to the Winnipiseogee Paper Company. The 233' long three-span viaduct became known as the Sulphite Bridge for its purpose of delivering sulphite-laden trains to the mills.

The Sulphite Bridge, at first glance, does not look like a typical covered bridge. But it is indeed a covered bridge, as the Pratt trusses, which support the rail bed, were covered. The railroad runs on the top of the roof instead of underneath, forming a deck truss instead of the conventional through truss. In reference to this design, the Sulphite Railroad Bridge is also referred to as the Upside-Down Bridge. The mills closed in 1933, and the railroad line was abandoned in 1973. On October 27, 1980, the Sulphite Bridge was significantly damaged due to a suspicious fire. Considered arson, the fire completely destroyed the siding and left only charred timbers spanning the Winnipesaukee. The roof and the tracks remain. The bridge can be accessed along the Winnipesaukee River Trail.

Fun Fact: The Sulphite Bridge sat alone over the river, largely unnoticed, even by residents who had walked the tracks over the river and claimed not to have realized that a covered bridge was below their feet. The covered bridge community didn't realize it either until the fall of 1965, when an article appeared in the National Society for the Preservation of Covered Bridges' October edition of Covered Bridge Topics. That article encouraged bridge enthusiasts and Franklin residents to visit the bridge.

Photo by Joseph Conwill, NSPCB Archives

Photo by Kim Chandler

Hamlet Railroad Bridge - Woonsocket, RI

Rhode Island is the only New England state without any historic covered bridges. The last one was the Hamlet Railroad Bridge built in 1898 by the New Haven Railroad on a spur line over the Blackstone River between Hamlet Village and the Social Mills area of Woonsocket. This crossing was the last historic covered bridge in Rhode Island. The bridge was a single span Howe truss with a pony truss approach span over an old power canal on the Hamlet end, and a long trestle approach on the Social Mills end. An interesting shaped roof covered a pedestrian walkway on the downstream side. In the 1950s, one train a day would pass over it to service the American Wiper-Waste Mill on Social Street. The bridge was destroyed by Hurricane Diane on August 19, 1955.

Woonsocket also had another covered railroad bridge called the Bandwagon Bridge. It was built for the Woonsocket and Pascoag Railroad in 1891, at the location of a former bridge washed away by floodwaters fifteen years earlier. An excursion of public and railway officials toured the line on February 5, 1891. Riding in the locomotive was Enoch G. Sweatt, the contractor who built the railroad and the bridge. A week later, it was open to general traffic. The bridge went up in flames on October 22, 1935. The blaze threatened the Crown Piece Dye Works, then was pushed across the river by high winds to level a large warehouse of the Bouvier Construction Co. A heat explosion then damaged the adjoining two-story brick building on Sayles Street, occupied by the Verhulst Combing Company. A temporary wooden bridge was built after the fire. In September 1941, a new steel span was erected by the New York, New Haven and Hartford Railroad. That bridge was also damaged during the 1955 hurricane.

Fun Fact: Woonsocket began as a collection of textile mills along the Blackstone River in the 1830s, and was incorporated as a city in 1888. The growing mills attracted French-Canadian immigrants to the area. In the 1920s, three-quarters of the city's population was French-Canadian with French language newspapers and radio programs.

Photo by Henry A. Gibson, NSPCB Archives

Bridge at the Green or Arlington Bridge - Arlington, VT

The 80-foot-long bridge was built over the Batten Kill about 2½ miles east of the New York state line in 1852. The presence of the West Arlington Methodist Church makes for a classic New England scene. In its early years, the bridge was blown off of its abutments and toppled into the river. Being too heavy to be lifted back, it was taken apart and rebuilt, then tied to the banks by iron rods. In 1979, the structure had major repairs done, including jacking and shoring of the wooden structure, adding floor beams, replacing the floor, repairing the abutments and the lower chord, and repairing or replacing of some truss members for the sum of $74,920.50. It was listed on the National Register of Historic Places on August 28, 1973.

Fun Fact: The house on the far left of the exterior photo was the home of Norman Rockwell from 1939 to 1953, and is where he created many of his famous paintings. The original structure dates back to 1792.

Photo by Joseph Conwill, NSPCB Archives

Photo from the Richard Sanders Allen Collection, NSPCB Archives

Green River Bridge - Green River, VT

The Green River Bridge was built over the river of the same name in the village of Green River, in the town of Guilford. It was built by Marcus Worden (1812-1906) of Guilford in 1873, to replace a bridge lost in the October 1869 flood. The road crossed on a temporary, crib-supported structure until the town could finance the new bridge. Some sources list the construction date as 1870. However, the Vermont Phoenix (Brattleboro) of January 31, 1873, announced that "The prospect now is that the people of Green River will have a good bridge at that place. The job of building the abutments is let to M. H. Day of Chesterfield, N. H., and the building of a covered bridge to Marcus Worden of Guilford."

On November 29, 1873, the Vermont Journal (Windsor) announced that the bridge "has at last been so far completed as to allow the passage of teams." Because of its remote location, it does not see the heavy traffic experienced at other covered bridges in the state. The bridge features a sign stating "Two dollars fine to drive on this bridge faster than a walk."

Fun Fact: Just upstream from the covered bridge is a 110-foot wide and 10.5-foot high crib dam made of hemlock logs, filled with stone, and capped with hemlock planks. The dam was initially constructed in 1811, probably to provide power for a combined paper and linseed oil mill owned by Jonah Cutting and his son-in-law, William Gregory. The dam has been rebuilt several times over the years after damage from floods and ice flows. Next to the dam are the remains of the Henry Stowe water-powered grist and saw mill. The mill was constructed in 1871, and destroyed by a fire in 1918.

Photo by Bob Watts

Lower or Cox Brook or Newell or Second Bridge - Northfield Falls, VT

Photo by Bill & Jenn Caswell

This bridge is the middle of three historic covered bridges within 1/3 of a mile on Cox Brook Road in Northfield Falls. All three bridges are thought to have been built in 1872. In the 1960s, the original stone abutments of this structure were faced with concrete when the roadway was strengthened with steel I-beams. All three of the bridges were added to the National Register of Historic Places in 1974.

There are a total of five covered bridges within the town of Northfield:
1. Station or Northfield Falls Bridge crossing Dog River (1872)
2. Lower or Cox Brook or Newell or Second Bridge crossing Cox Brook (1872)
3. Third or Upper Cox Brook crossing Cox Brook (c1872)
4. Slaughter-House Bridge crossing Dog River (1872)
5. Moseley or Stony Brook Bridge crossing Stony Brook (1899).

The names of the builders of these structures are not yet known.

Fun Fact: There are only a few places in addition to Northfield Falls where two covered bridges can be seen together:

- North Hartland, Vermont
- The East Paden and West Paden bridges of Columbia County, Pennsylvania
- The Smolen-Gulf and Riverview bridges of Ashtabula County, Ohio
- A pair south of Mont-Laurier, Québec - Grand pont de Ferme Rouge and Petit pont de Ferme Rouge

North Hartland Twin Bridges - Hartland, VT

The twin covered bridges of North Hartland can be seen from Interstate 91, which is in the background of this photo. The West Twin Bridge is on the left and the East Twin on the right. The East Twin Bridge is also known as the Willard Bridge in honor of the family who owned the surrounding land. The land was sold to Oliver Brothers (1839-1919), who built the Ottauquechee Woolen Mill. The great flood of November 1927 spared the two bridges at this location although the mill building was wrecked. That flood is thought to have destroyed as many as one-third of the covered bridges standing in Vermont at the time. The shorter West Twin Bridge was lost during the 1938 hurricane and replaced by a concrete structure. That bridge was, in turn, replaced by a new covered bridge built by Jan Lewandoski of Greensboro Bend, Vermont, in 2001. The new structure was constructed in a nearby field and then moved into place. It features eighteen ship's knees used as braces near the top of the trusses. Sixteen of the eighteen ship's knees were cut from the stumps of tamarack trees, and the remaining two were cut from spruce stumps. The curvature where the root meets the stump provides a naturally strong roof brace.

Fun Fact: Oliver Brothers' obituary noted that he received a "substantial sum" of money for a patent on spinning jacks used in woolen mills in 1872. He used this windfall to purchase the land and construct the Ottauquechee Woolen Mill in North Hartland. It also mentioned that he invented a "labor-saving street sweeper" used in Worcester, Massachusetts.

Photo by Jenn Caswell Photo

Sanborn Bridge - Lyndonville, VT

While the bridge's portal carries an 1867 date, other construction dates such as, 1869 and 1873, have been offered for the bridge. It was originally built on Center Street in Lyndonville over the Passumpsic River. The bridge was partially destroyed by flooding in June 1926. It was added to the National Register of Historic Places on June 20, 1974.

In 2013, there was concern that the bridge was in danger of collapsing, due to a number of broken structural members. The National Society for the Preservation of Covered Bridges contributed funds to stabilize the structure. Tim Andrews of Barns & Bridges of New England made the repairs during the fall and winter of 2013. At the time, a full restoration was estimated at $1.2 million. In January 2022, the Town of Lyndon received a $100,000 grant towards that work and purchased the bridge from its owners.

Fun Fact: At the town meeting in March 1960, the voters decided to have the bridge replaced. To save it from demolition, Mr. and Mrs. Armand Morin purchased the structure for one dollar. They bought a lot of land adjacent to their Lynburke Motel and hired Milton Graton and Sons to move it about a mile through Lyndonville to its present location, near the intersection of routes 5 and 112. The move required removal and replacement of utility wires, and at one corner, a tree was dug up so the bridge could fit through and then replanted afterward.

Photo by Richard E. Roy, NSPCB Archives

Village or Maple Street or Lower Bridge - Farifax, VT

This single-span bridge was built over Mill Brook in Fairfax, Vermont, in 1865, by Kingsbury & Stone. It is unusually wide for a small historic covered bridge. This was likely to accommodate two-way traffic in the village. It was listed on the National Register of Historic Places on November 4, 1974. Following damage caused by a truck driver, the bridge was repaired in 2002, by Jan Lewendoski.

Franklin County has eight remaining covered bridges, with five of them in the town of Montgomery. Many of the standing and former covered bridges in the area were built by two brothers, Sheldon (1842-1889) and Savanard Jewett (1848-1925). Savanard's name is often misspelled as Savannah. The Comstock, Hutchins and West Hill Bridges, all built in Montgomery in 1883, are remaining examples of their work. Timber for their bridges was often cut from the family farm in the West Hill area of Montgomery and processed at their own lumber mill.

Fun Fact: During the great flood of November 1927, this bridge was washed off its abutments. Some say that when it was set back into place, it was positioned with its east end facing west.

Photo by Henry A. Gibson, NSPCB Archives

ILLUSTRATOR

Courtney Parsons

Courtney Parsons is an illustrator, graphic designer, and a free-lance artist hailing from Laconia, New Hampshire. Above all, she is a nature admirer and an animal lover, both being prominent themes throughout much of her artistic work. Currently, Courtney resides in Northern Virginia, where she works, attends George Mason University, and lives with her fiancé and cat. Courtney has a deep-rooted fondness for the beautiful Lakes Region, and she considers it an honor to be involved in this project with Heidi and the entire team at Give a Salute!.

COLLABORATOR

Heidi Smith

Heidi Smith is a native of New Hampshire's Lakes Region, where she raised her son and still resides. She has spent the majority of her professional career in the local health care setting, celebrating over 37 years.

Her passion for history has led her to many opportunities, one of which is the coloring book series, *Color Your Way USA*. This began after she noticed Courtney Parsons' online drawing of the Colonial Theatre, which is located in Heidi's hometown. Once she saw the illustration, she knew a coloring book series featuring different historical locations throughout the country needed to be created.

Along with Courtney and the staff of Give a Salute!, Heidi and the team put this concept into design, and they are now collaborating with several nonprofits to help raise money for those organizations as a unique way to preserve and interact with history.

We hope you have enjoyed coloring your way through the Covered Bridges of New England, and you have learned a little about its past.

To find out how to color your way through your own community's history, we invite you to contact **Give a Salute!** at **giveasalute@gmail.com.** Also visit our website: **htttp://giveasalute.com.**